Possum Poo

First published 2025
Published by: Bedford Books
ABN 32 847 640 702

All rights reserved. No part of this publication may be reproduced in any form
without permission from the publisher, except as permitted by the Australian copyright law.
For permission contact: read@bedfordbooks.com.au

National Library of Australia Cataloguing-in-Publication entry:

 A catalogue record for this
book is available from the
National Library of Australia

Author: Helen Koekemoer
Illustrator: Janet Freeman
Title: Possum Poo

ISBN: 978-1-7643739-0-6 (hardback)
ISBN: 978-1-7643739-1-3 (softback)
ISBN: 978-1-7643739-2-0 (E-Book)

Target audience: Children
Creative non-fiction
Mostly truthfulness with minor creativity
Artwork: Hand illustrated and hand painted

Possum Poo

Dedicated to:
Anton, Aimee and Darryl

Author- Helen Koekemoer
Illustrator - Janet Freeman

Slam went the shed door.
Darkness fell.

The school bell clanged as the children
scrambled onto the bus.
It was late on Friday afternoon, and
the children were on their way home
after a hot and humid day.

The bus clambered down the road,
packed with chatty children
looking forward to a fun filled weekend.

On Friday the children wanted to play.

Gingerly, they opened the shed and hooray!

Blossom was trapped in a cage. But in a terrible rage.

About the Author
Helen Koekemoer was born in South Africa, is married and has two children and four grandchildren.
She lives in Queensland, Australia with her husband.

Helen is passionate about early childhood education and is a primary school teacher.
She has a double degree in Education, as well as qualifications in Speech Pathology and Educare.
Her interests include photography, baking, exploring the outdoors, wildlife, visual art and writing.

Helen has a heart for young learners and desires to inspire children to develop
an enjoyment of reading through her **true stories.**

About the Illustrator
Janet Freeman began her creative journey in advertising agencies and design studios in both
South Africa and Mauritius. Her lifelong passion for visual art has been enriched by countless visits to
art galleries and a keen interest in the history of art.

In this book, she hopes to bring that passion to life through simple, engaging illustrations designed
to inspire children to explore and enjoy art and reading.

Beyond her professional life, Janet enjoys painting, poetry, designing personalised cards,
and spending treasured time with her grandchildren.

www.ingramcontent.com/pod-product-compliance
Lightning Source LLC
Chambersburg PA
CBHW041644220426
43661CB00018B/1297